Do You Know Dewey?

For librarians everywhere —B. P. C.

For Maarten, Max, and Mattiece: thank you
for being the best part of my life —J. L.-V.

The publisher wishes to thank Liz
Deskins, Teacher-Librarian, J.W. Reason
Elementary School, Hilliard, Ohio;
Betsy Smith, Library Information
Specialist, Orange Grove Elementary,
Seminole, Florida; and Carole
Weitzel, Librarian, Lois F. Giddens
Elementary School, Cedar Park,
Texas, for sharing their wisdom
about the finer points of the
Dewey decimal system.

Text copyright © 2013 by Brian P. Cleary
Illustrations copyright © 2013 by Joanne Lew-Vriethoff

Millbrook Press
A division of Lerner Publishing Group, Inc.
241 First Avenue North
Minneapolis, MN 55401 U.S.A.

Website address: www.lernerbooks.com

Main body text set in Quay Sans ITC Std.
Typeface provided by ITC.

Library of Congress Cataloging-in-Publication Data

Cleary, Brian P., 1959–
Do you know Dewey? : exploring the Dewey decimal system
/ by Brian P. Cleary ; illustrated by Joanne Lew-Vriethoff.
   pages   cm
   ISBN: 978–0–7613–6676–8 (lib. bdg.)
   1. Classification, Dewey decimal—Juvenile literature.
   I. Lew-Vriethoff, Joanne, illustrator. II. Title.
Z696.D7C58 2013
025.4'31—dc23   2011046168

Manufactured in the United States of America
1 – PC – 7/15/12

Do You Know Dewey?

Exploring the Dewey Decimal System

BRIAN P. CLEARY

illustrations by JOANNE LEW-VRIETHOFF

M Millbrook Press • Minneapolis

Melvil Dewey loved to read
when he was very small,

but libraries
were so mixed up,
they brought
no joy at all.

And that's why little Melvil would grow up to make a system to organize those stacks of books and classify and list 'em.

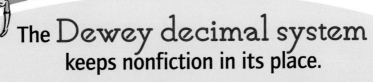

The Dewey decimal system
keeps nonfiction in its place.

Books are grouped by subject, such as art or outer space.

This system mainly covers books on topics that are real:

people, things, and places jammed with factual appeal!

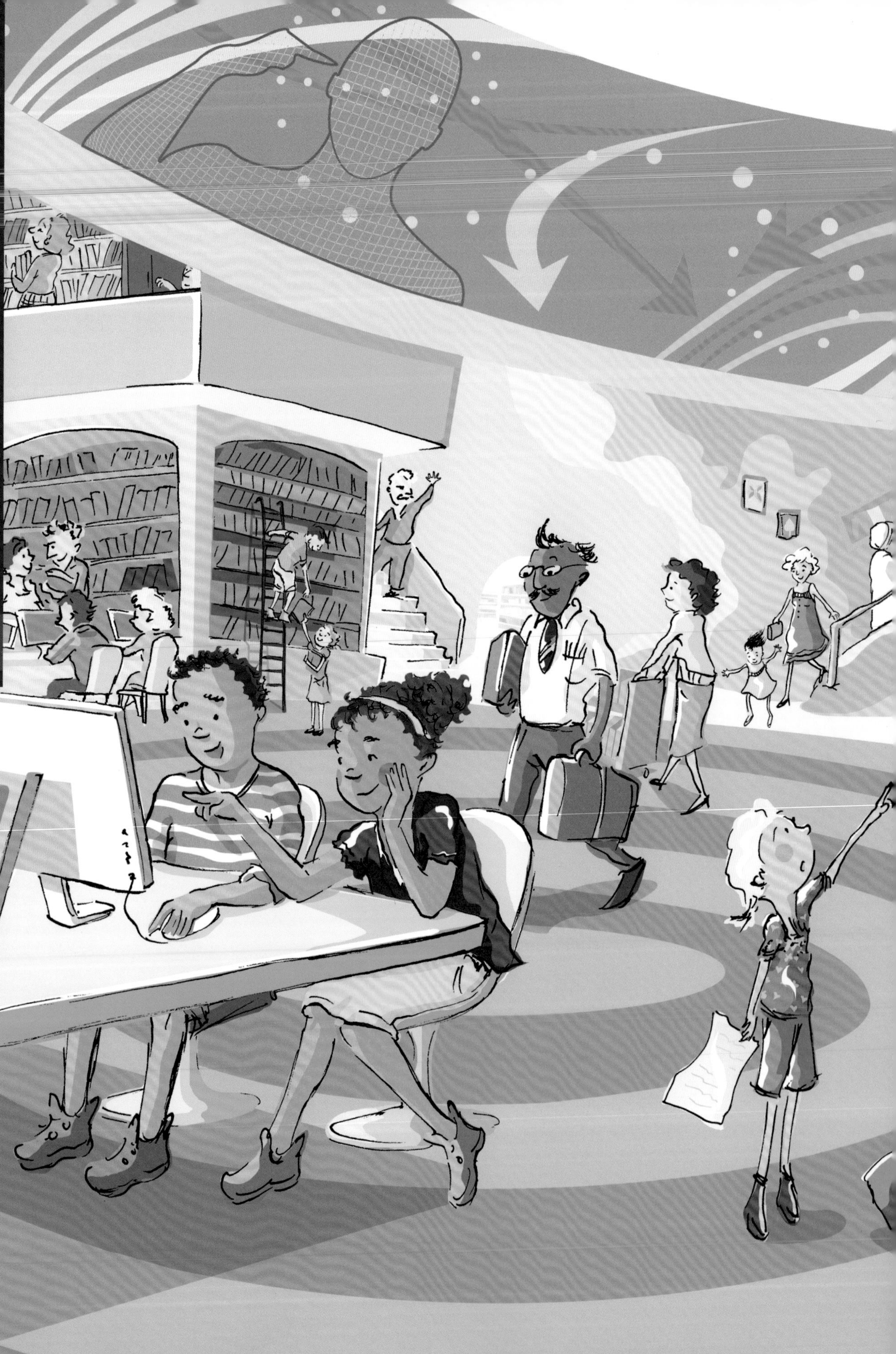

For instance, if you're searching for a book all by yourself

about the Internet, you wouldn't look on every shelf.

Instead, you'd check the numbers at the ends of all the rows.

You want the section labeled with the zeroes, or the Os.

The section marked 100s is the one that you'd look through

to find a book that tells us why we act the way we do.

It offers books explaining dreams and feelings. Others tell of optical illusions or of places ghosts may dwell.

Walk through the 200s, and you'll find religion here.

Holy books for Christians, Muslims, Jews, and more appear.

There are books to help you study, understand, and probe beliefs and faiths of people living all around the globe.

Social sciences are next, and this 300s section's

got topics such as government and money and elections,

scouting and the military,
books on education,

customs, costumes, etiquette,
and also transportation.

In shelves marked with 400s,
you'll see books of every kind

on language—from the written
and the spoken to the signed.

Look up hieroglyphics
and discover what they mean.

Perhaps they'll lead you to the tomb
of some Egyptian queen!

All of the 500s cover science and mathematics—
perfect for both chemistry and algebra fanatics,
along with those enthusiasts of weather, birds, and bees,
dinosaurs, volcanoes,
stars and oceans,
plants and trees.

But what about inventions?
Pets? Our bodies and disease?

Or cooking? The 600s
is the home for all of these.

Want to know about the parts
in each kitchen appliance?

For all of this and spaceships too,
look here in applied science!

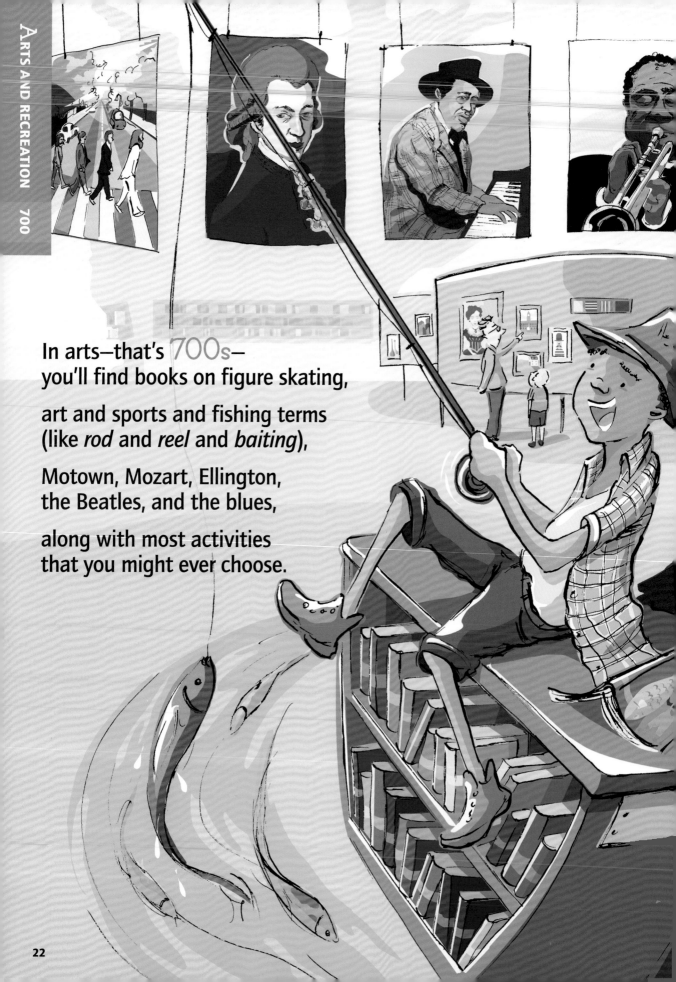

In arts—that's 700s—
you'll find books on figure skating,

art and sports and fishing terms
(like *rod* and *reel* and *baiting*),

Motown, Mozart, Ellington,
the Beatles, and the blues,

along with most activities
that you might ever choose.

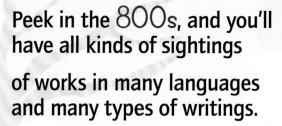

Peek in the 800s, and you'll have all kinds of sightings

of works in many languages and many types of writings.

Here, speeches, plays, and poetry—with something for all ages—

along with puns and silly jokes and riddles fill the pages.

What's in the 900s? It isn't any mystery.
That's where you would look for both geography and history,
biography and travel, flags and maps of all the nations,
tales of knights and castles and exciting explorations.

The Dewey decimal system
uses each distinct division

to help you find nonfiction books
with speed and with precision.

So let the numbers lead you
as they guide you through each zone,

and you'll be set to travel
on some journeys of your own!

How can you use the Dewey decimal system to find a book at the library? You have two choices. Let's say you want to find a book about dogs. As you read earlier, books about pets (including dogs) are in the 600s section. So you could go to that section and start looking at books. Or you could use your library's online catalog. You might look up the subject *dogs.* The catalog will give you a list of books about dogs. It will also give you the call number for each book.

A call number is like an address for a book. Your address makes it easy to find your house in your city. A call number makes it easy to find a book in a library.

A book's call number is on a label on its spine. It is a three-digit number. There may also be a decimal point and more numbers after the three-digit number. Each digit tells you something about the book. For example, let's look at a book with the call number 636.75 CLE. Here is what each number in the call number stands for:

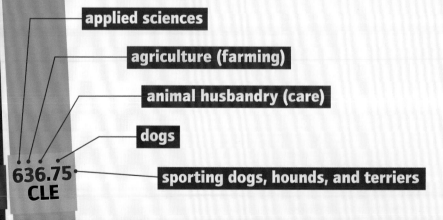

applied sciences

agriculture (farming)

animal husbandry (care)

dogs

636.75 CLE

sporting dogs, hounds, and terriers

The letters after the number are the first few letters of the author's last name. (For biographies, which are in the 900s section, the call number uses the first few letters of the *subject's* last name.)

The call number's first digit tells you which hundreds section of the library to look in. The rest of the number tells you where within the section to find the book. Look at the range of call numbers posted at the end of each bookshelf to figure out exactly which shelf to go to. The books on each shelf are organized in numerical order. As you look at a bookshelf, the book with the smallest number is at the top left and the book with the biggest number is at the bottom right.

When Melvil Dewey created the Dewey decimal system, he included places for works of nonfiction and fiction. The section for the fiction is the 800s. But in most modern libraries, the novels and fictional picture books are shelved separately from the nonfiction. The fiction section no longer uses Dewey call numbers. Instead, fiction books are organized in alphabetical order by the author's last name.

Knowing the Dewey decimal system is like knowing a secret code. Suddenly the numbers and letters don't seem so random. Instead, they're hints that get you closer and closer to what you want to find out about!

600-699

The Dewey Decimal System

000 – Computer science, information, and general works

100 – Philosophy and psychology

200 – Religion

300 – Social sciences

400 – Language

500 – Science

600 – Applied science (technology)

700 – Arts and recreation

800 – Literature

900 – History and geography